TIME FOR KIDS READERS

What's the Weather?

by Alan M. Ruben

 Harcourt

Orlando   Austin   Chicago   New York   Toronto   London   San Diego

Visit *The Learning Site!*
www.harcourtschool.com

On some days the sun shines.

2

On some days the wind **blows**.

On some days it **rains**.

On some days it **snows**.

Will the sun shine **today**?

Get ready for rain.

What is the weather **now**?